I0762763

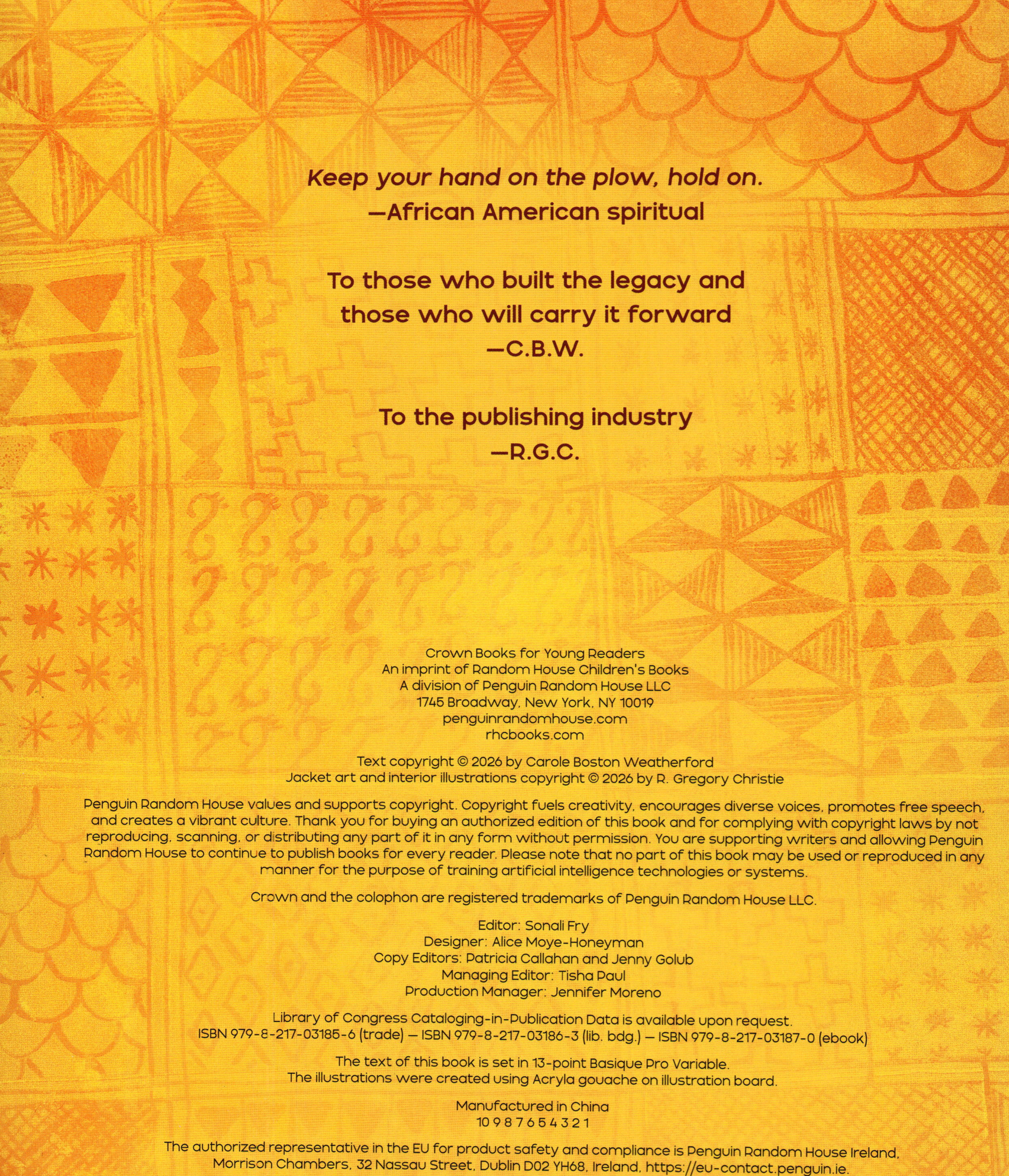

Keep your hand on the plow, hold on.
—African American spiritual

To those who built the legacy and
those who will carry it forward
—C.B.W.

To the publishing industry
—R.G.C.

Crown Books for Young Readers
An imprint of Random House Children's Books
A division of Penguin Random House LLC
1745 Broadway, New York, NY 10019
penguinrandomhouse.com
rhcbooks.com

Editor: Sonali Fry
Designer: Alice Moye-Honeyman
Copy Editors: Patricia Callahan and Jenny Golub
Managing Editor: Tisha Paul
Production Manager: Jennifer Moreno

Library of Congress Cataloging-in-Publication Data is available upon request.
ISBN 979-8-217-03185-6 (trade) — ISBN 979-8-217-03186-3 (lib. bdg.) — ISBN 979-8-217-03187-0 (ebook)

The text of this book is set in 13-point Basique Pro Variable.
The illustrations were created using Acryla gouache on illustration board.

Manufactured in China
10 9 8 7 6 5 4 3 2 1

The authorized representative in the EU for product safety and compliance is Penguin Random House Ireland, Morrison Chambers, 32 Nassau Street, Dublin D02 YH68, Ireland, https://eu-contact.penguin.ie.

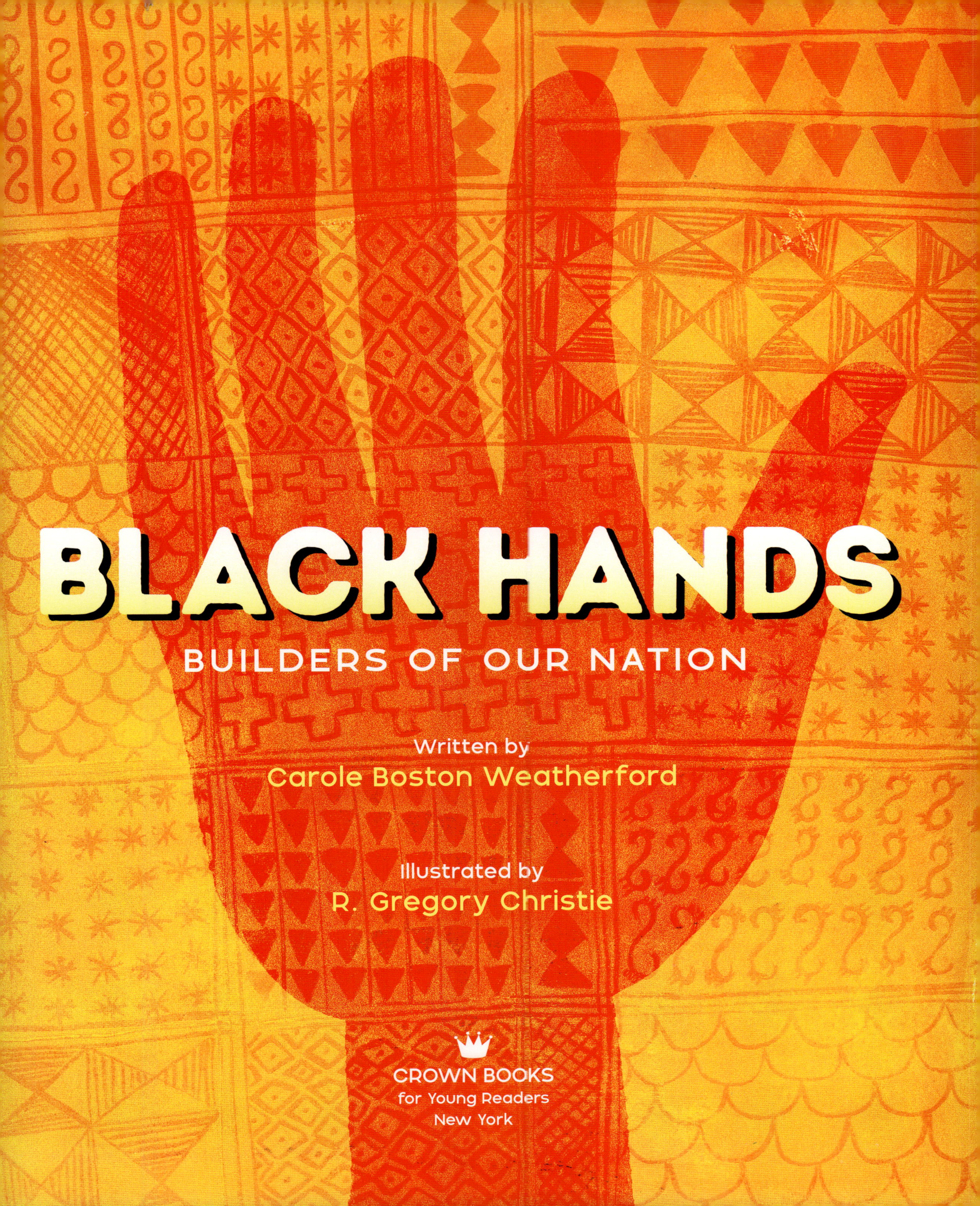

BLACK HANDS

BUILDERS OF OUR NATION

Written by
Carole Boston Weatherford

Illustrated by
R. Gregory Christie

CROWN BOOKS
for Young Readers
New York

Black hands, clutching memories of Africa,
survived the Middle Passage
and arrived in the Americas,
only to face the auction block.

Black hands reached for
kinfolk being sold away.
Black hands prayed.

Oh!
Didn't we pray!

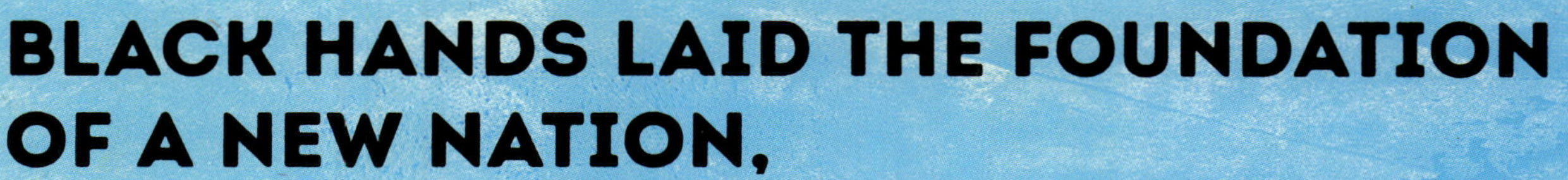

BLACK HANDS LAID THE FOUNDATION OF A NEW NATION,

forged iron for gates closed to them,
and built the White House and the Capitol,
story by story, stone by stone.

Black hands stitched quilts and flags

and fashioned ball gowns
for First Ladies.

Black hands wove baskets of sweetgrass and willow.

Black hands took leavings and slim pickings
and simmered them into soul food,

flavors that generations would savor.

BLACK HANDS
BROKE
THE CHAINS.

Black hands took up arms in every American war.

Black hands had to fight
for every single right.

BLACK HANDS PLOWED THIS LAND,

planted seeds of change,
and harvested new hope every day.

Black hands cleared the wilderness
to make way for farms.
Black hands grew tobacco, rice,
indigo, sugarcane, and cotton.

Black hands herded cattle
and busted broncos.

Black hands drove spikes and laid tracks.

Black hands
engineered innovations
that made industry
hummmmmm.

Black hands beat drums and plucked banzas—
banjos that put the twang in roots music.
Black hands set the tempo for ragtime
and strummed the blues into being.

Black hands jammed jazz!

Black hands clutched microphones
that amplified fresh voices, bold sounds.
Black hands applauded shining stars.

BLACK HANDS PENNED
LITERARY TESTAMENTS
that have stood the test of time.

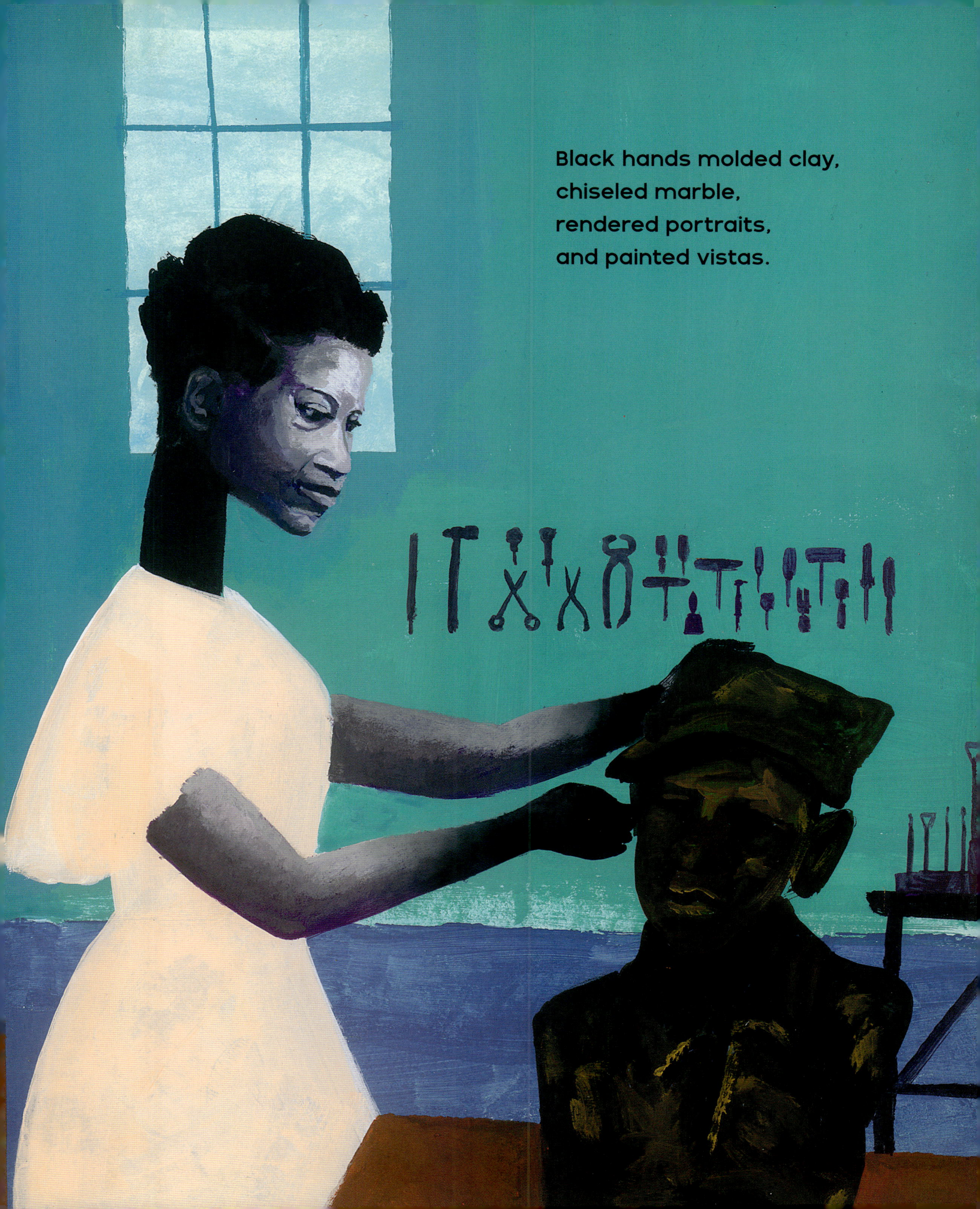

Black hands molded clay,
chiseled marble,
rendered portraits,
and painted vistas.

Black hands sought cures and healed sickness.

BLACK HANDS CARESSED, COMFORTED,

AND CONSOLED.

Black hands clapped to spirituals
and beat tambourines to gospel hymns.
Black hands prayed.

Oh!
Didn't we pray!

Black hands gripped satchels full of faith
and left the rural South for big cities

and bigger dreams.

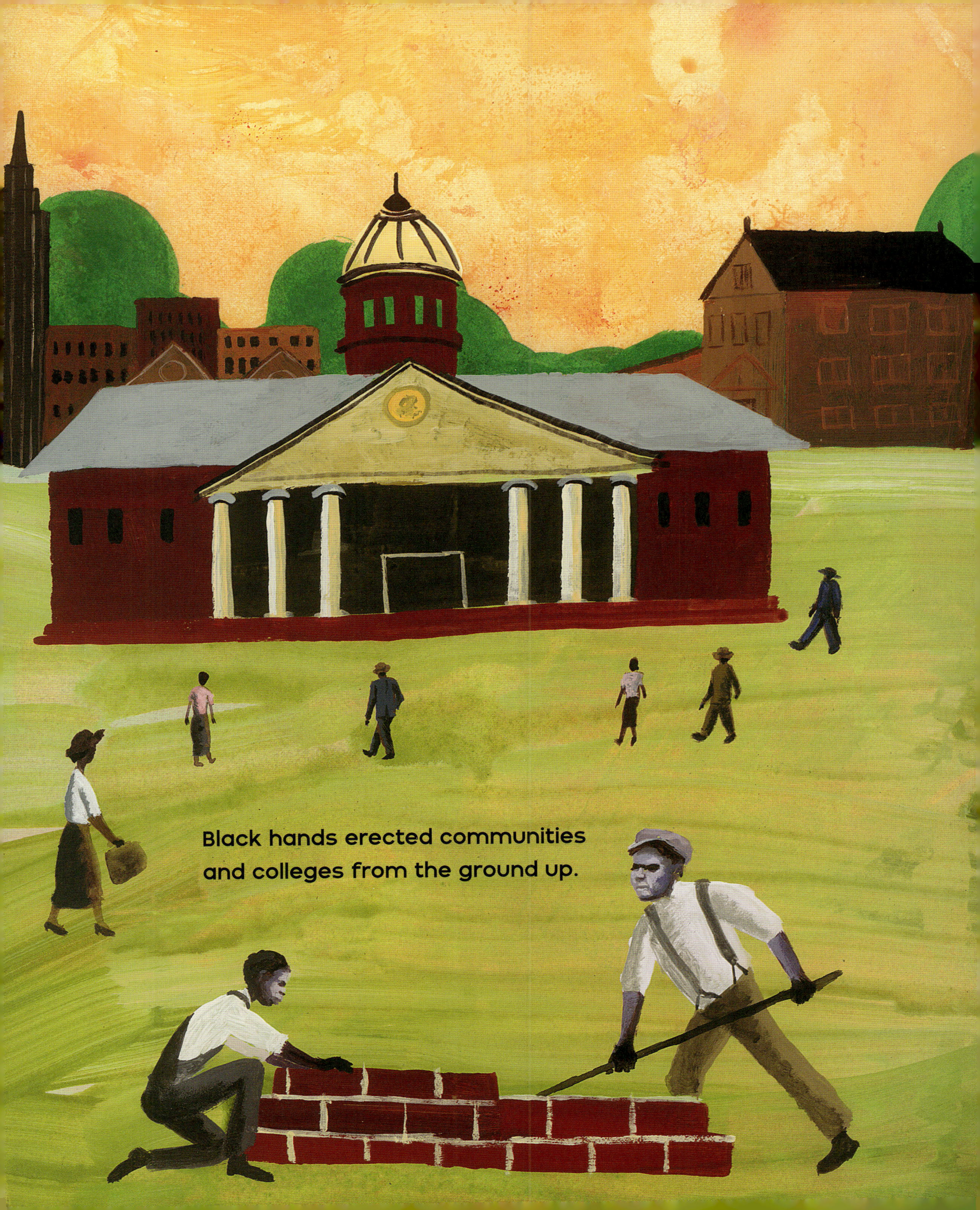

Black hands erected communities
and colleges from the ground up.

Black hands predicted eclipses

and plotted the stars
and voyages to the moon.

BLACK HANDS PUSHED OPEN CLOSED DOORS

and pulled back the curtains on injustice.

Black hands raised picket signs

and joined together
to march for equality.

Black hands scored victories and shattered records, passing the baton on down.

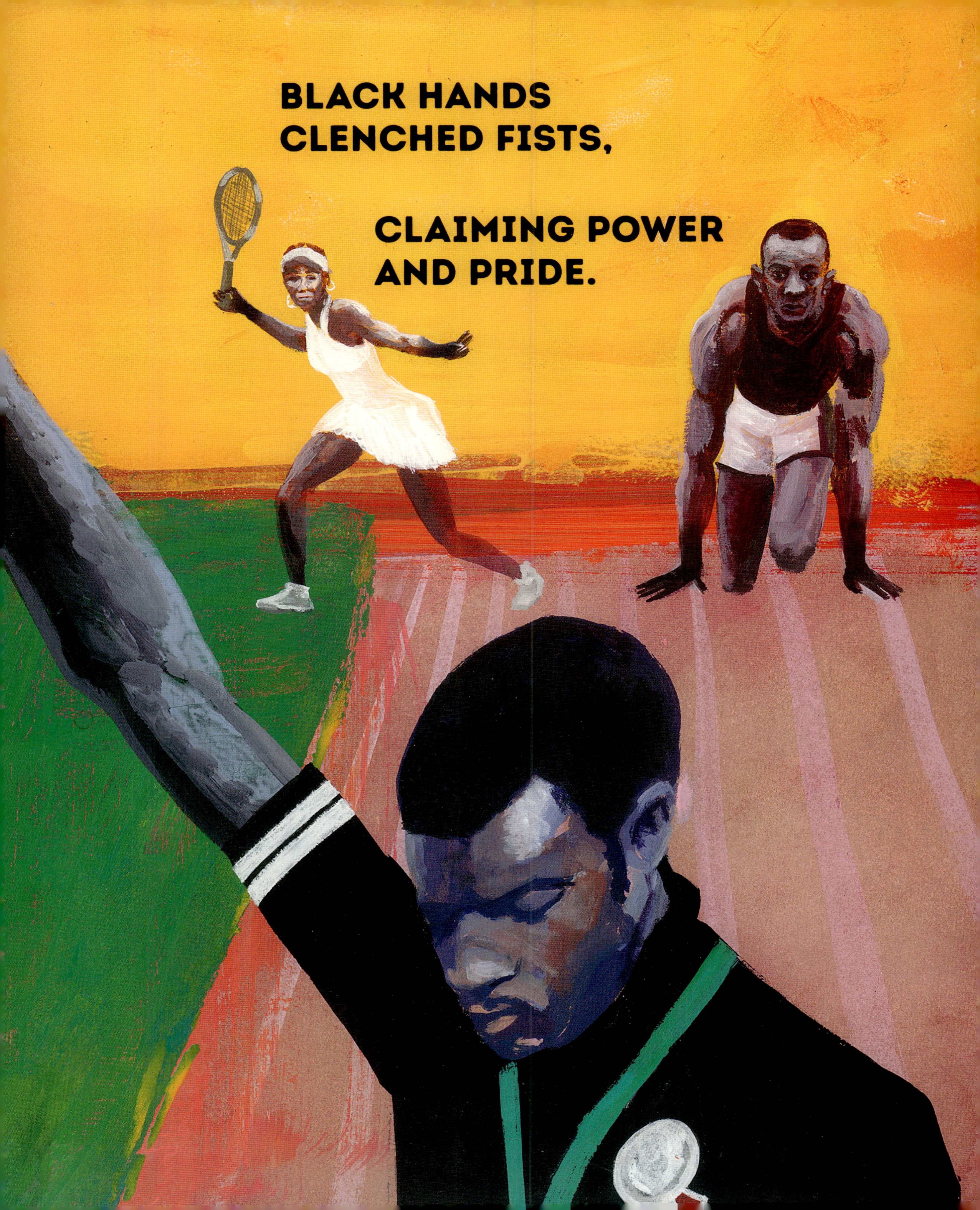
BLACK HANDS
CLENCHED FISTS,
CLAIMING POWER
AND PRIDE.

BLACK HANDS WENT UP
TO SAY THAT WE MATTER.

Black hands cast ballots, electing legislators, mayors, governors, and presidents.

Black hands pounded gavels to lay down the law.

BLACK HANDS POINT THE WAY FOR MORE TO FOLLOW.

Black hands uplift the young, who own tomorrow.

Black hands hold strong through struggle,
prodding this land to live up to its promise:

**LIBERTY
AND JUSTICE
FOR ALL.**

★★★ HISTORICAL REFERENCES ★★★

THE MIDDLE PASSAGE: This is the route that was used to send ships of enslaved people from Africa to the New World. After arriving, these people endured harsh punishments. They were separated from their families, sold and stripped of their identities, forced to work grueling jobs for no pay, and denied basic freedoms.

ENSLAVED ARTISANS: Enslaved African Americans had specialized skills that were undervalued and exploited. For instance, some wove sweetgrass baskets in the West African tradition that are now considered treasured works of art. Enslaved laborers also helped to construct US landmarks such as the White House and the Capitol building.

HARRIET TUBMAN (1822–1913): An abolitionist who escaped enslavement and led approximately seventy people to freedom via the Underground Railroad, a network of antislavery activists and safe houses. She also served as a nurse, scout, and spy for the Union Army during the Civil War, risking her life to fight for freedom.

THE 102ND COLORED INFANTRY REGIMENT: Originally formed in 1863 and called the First Michigan Colored Infantry Regiment, this unit consisted largely of African American volunteers. Despite facing racism, they served in the Civil War, showing courage and helping the Union win, thus contributing to the end of slavery.

SHARECROPPING: After the Civil War, many newly freed African Americans became sharecroppers, farmers who rented small plots of land from plantation owners in exchange for a share of crops. Sharecropping was often just as oppressive as slavery, forcing people to work in harsh conditions and keeping them in debt.

COWBOYS: During the late nineteenth century, approximately 25 percent of the cowboys in the West were African Americans. Most were newly freed men who worked as ranch hands and cattle drivers. Legendary African American cowboys included Bill Pickett and Nat Love.

MUSIC: Many music genres—including blues, gospel, jazz, rock and roll, and hip-hop—stem from African traditions and African American spirituals. Spirituals blended African musical elements with Christian themes, serving as both worship and resistance, along with work songs, field hollers, and other Black musical expressions.

THE HARLEM RENAISSANCE: A cultural, social, and artistic movement during the 1920s and 1930s in Harlem—a neighborhood in New York City—that celebrated African American cultural expressions. A large number of African Americans established roots in Harlem, such as writers Zora Neale Hurston and Langston Hughes and sculptor Augusta Savage.

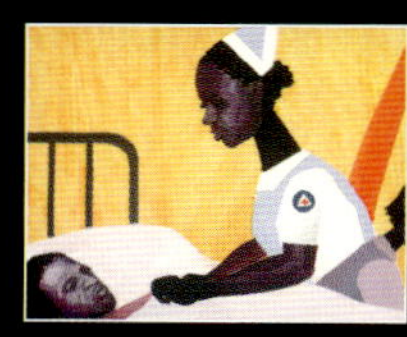

WORLD WAR II NURSES: During World War II, there were about five hundred African American nurses, who were restricted to serving in segregated hospitals and aid stations and providing medical care for German prisoners of war. They faced discrimination but displayed courage and skill, contributing greatly to the war effort.

THE GREAT MIGRATION: Poverty and racism drove more than six million African Americans from their homes in the South to towns and cities across America. Many headed to big cities like New York, Chicago, and Philadelphia, seeking better housing and employment opportunities.

HISTORICALLY BLACK COLLEGES AND UNIVERSITIES: Now called HBCUs, these institutions were established to provide quality education for African American students during times of segregation. HBCUs like Howard University, Spelman College, and Morehouse College are symbols of academic excellence.

SPACE EXPLORATION: African Americans have contributed to scientific advancements in fields such as space exploration. Mathematician Katherine Johnson's calculations were essential to NASA's early space missions. And Mae Jemison, as a NASA astronaut, became the first African American woman to travel in space in 1992.

THE NATIONAL ASSOCIATION OF COLORED WOMEN'S CLUBS (NACWC): This organization was established in 1896 to advocate for a wide range of reforms to improve life for African Americans. It was founded by African American suffragists, who were often left out of the predominantly white national suffragist movement.

AFRICAN AMERICAN ATHLETES: Trailblazing African American athletes have included Florence "Flo-Jo" Griffith Joyner, who set world records in track and field; tennis player Serena Williams, who won twenty-three Grand Slam titles; Jesse Owens, who won four gold medals at the 1936 Berlin Olympics; and Tommie Smith, who made the Black Power salute by raising his fist in silent protest when he won gold in the 200-meter sprint at the 1968 Olympics.

DR. MARTIN LUTHER KING, JR. (1929–1968): A prominent leader of the Civil Rights Movement who organized peaceful mass protests that helped to end segregation and gain important rights for African Americans. He inspired millions with his oration, including the famous "I Have a Dream" speech.

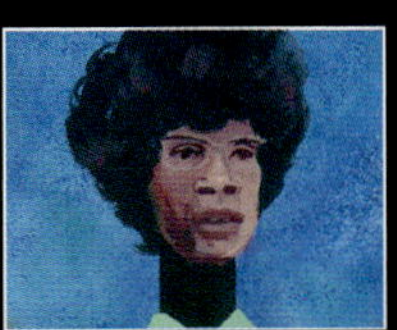

SHIRLEY CHISHOLM (1924–2005): The first African American woman in Congress, she served seven terms as a New York representative from 1969 to 1983. In 1972, she was also the first woman and African American to seek a major party's nomination to run for president of the United States.

THE 1ST RHODE ISLAND REGIMENT: A unit in the American colonies' Continental Army during the Revolutionary War, formed in 1778 and also known as the Black Regiment. Notable for being one of the first regiments to enlist African American and Native American soldiers, it played a significant role in several key battles, including the Battle of Rhode Island in 1778.

JULY 4, 1776: Celebrations of the founding of the United States—such as the commemoration in 2026 of the signing of the Declaration of Independence 250 years earlier—are good times to come together and reflect on the contributions of the underrepresented throughout American history.